THE PICTORIAL GUIDE TO GROUP WORK ACTIVITIES

VOLUME ONE

GEOFF SANDERS

Acknowledgements.

Thanks to all those people who have contributed ideas and offered assistance and encouragement in the creation of this book, with particular thanks to Janet Neesam, Simon Newbronner, Nick Lister, Phill Barnett and all the staff at 'Cita'. and Outward Bound © Wales

Contents.

For ease of reference the activities have been grouped into the following sections. However the sections are not exclusive and many games are transferable.

Once upon a time....

1. .... all the books about group work activities were extremely boring & tedious.... ...UNTIL

Wouldn't it be great to produce a picture book of games that is easy to understand?

2. It would draw on our experiences in professional training & working....

3. ...... with youth & adults in the city.

4. Who's the book aimed at?

5. Anybody wishing to introduce stimulating activities to their work with groups.

6. The reader will see each game acted out in a comic strip story making the book both fun & easy to use.

Amazing!

Introduction.

If you want to extend your knowledge of group work activities so that it includes a complete range of some of the best ideas around, you need look no further than this unique pictorial book.

By the use of explicit cartoon drawings the need for lengthy written descriptions and pages of laborious reading has been eliminated.

Each activity is presented in the form of a short comicstrip story which is based on the observations of the games in practise. The layout of each page and the sequential action drawings are designed to achieve maximum visual clarity and understanding of the purpose of each game. The viewer is able to flip through each section with ease to select appropriate material.

Material for this book has been collected over a number of years, and many experienced group workers in the fields of Social Work, Youth Work, Education and Development Training have contributed valuable ideas. These can be used constructively with a broad spectrum of Youth Groups, and can be of particular interest for those working with adults in areas of Personal, Team and Management Development.

This is not a theoretical work but together the games comprehensively cover the aspects of group work commonly employed, ranging from 'Warm Up' and 'Ice-Breakers', that last a few minutes, through to more challenging activities which may last several hours.

Some new variations on well known themes have been included together with a number of exciting original ideas that are appearing for the first time in book form.

As a part of a group work programme these activities can assist individuals and groups to function more effectively at work or school and in their social lives. This is possible because they engage people on a number of different levels. They are purposeful, provide tangible results and a focus for discussion during a review.

Although only games they involve some physical reality, e.g. get over an obstacle or find a location. To achieve these objectives the group will of necessity become involved in physical action, thought and emotion. They can also be a great deal of fun which may be reason enough for doing some of them.

All of the activities have been tried and tested many times. They are often developments of earlier ideas and may be adapted according to individual needs and circumstances. The possibilities for this are limitless and this book hopes to add to this evolutionary process.

All of the games and exercises should be properly supervised by responsible persons who can make a judgement about the suitability and safety aspects relating to any particular group

The author and publishers cannot be held responsible in any way for any accidents or injuries that may occur during the course of these activities.

q

Warm Up.

The activities in the opening section are all of short duration, active and fun. They require minimum preparation or equipment and are particularly suited for use with groups that are meeting for the first time. Use them to stimulate verbal and physical interaction before moving on to a more challenging activity.

By working together to achieve a simple task, members of the newly formed group are encouraged to establish contact and to overcome some of their initial inhibitions.

The first game is probably the best known of the many 'name games' but it is followed by a useful extention which is not nearly so well known.

Group leaders may consider that certain contact exercises may not be suitable for use with some mixed sex groups.

Name Game.

In a circle. Each person states their name in turn. A ball is then thrown at random around the group, — the thrower calling the name of the catcher.

The caller must now make 2 consecutive throws to the left calling names & then repeat this to the right.

11

Name Game 2.

1. Once everybody has had a chance to learn each others names, one person is blindfolded.

2. One other person quietly leaves the room.

3. Everyone else swops places or . . . .

4. . . . . distributes themselves around the room. The first person removes the blindfold & must name & describe the missing person.

Follow Me.

1."Stand on the far side of the room & put on blindfolds."

2."Now everybody walk towards the sound of my voice."

3. NOTE: Once everybody has started towards you, move around the room while continuing to talk.

4."O.K. blindfolds off now. Tell the person nearest to you 3 things about yourself."

Caterpillar.

The person at the far end is going to roll across the others.....

....then stop on reaching this end.

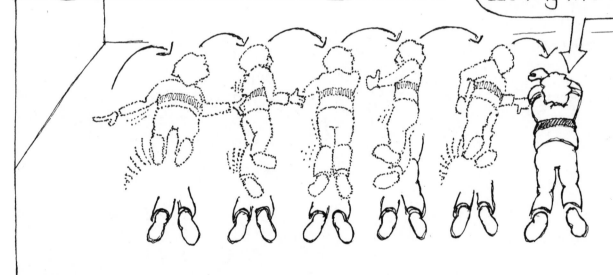

The next person repeats the process & so on down the line.

Human Machine.

Human alphabet.

Divide the group into 2s or 3s. Now call out letters of the alphabet at random.

Each unit must form the letter called using all its members.

A.

F.

K.

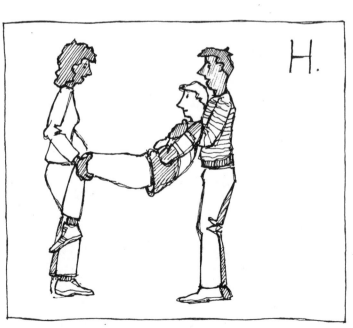

H.

Contact Points.

Tangle.

1. In a circle...

2. ...link hands across, using different people for each hand.

3. ...Now untangle yourselves without letting go of hands.

Scramble.

Two magazines are cut down the middle. All the pages are mixed up. The group reform them...

...within a time limit.

Stop the Leak.

You have 5 minutes to fill the bucket with water, without moving it. Only use that (remote) water supply and these 2 cups.

Plastic container with various sized holes.

Elevator.

Individuals are taken one at a time to a location which is out of sight from the rest of the group.

1.

Put this blindfold on & stand on the plank.

2. Supporter.

We're going to lift you up to touch the ceiling. Your supporter will steady you if needed.

3.

NOTE: We only raise the plank by a few inches.

4.

Touch the head with a 2nd plank to create the feeling of elevation.

5. O.K. you're down.

The first time I saw this exercise the person being lifted was deliberately tipped off the plank when they thought they had reached the ceiling. Only those who had been on the elevator were allowed to observe. All thought it was hilarious.

Lace Up.

Trust.

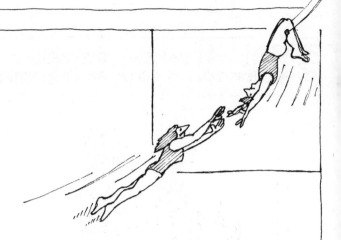

In order to achieve good working relationships it is important that the group establishes a basis of trust and a feeling of security between individual members. The following activities develop this by making the group responsible for the physical security of each person in turn.

Very little or no equipment is required and most of the activities are of short duration, i.e. a few minutes.

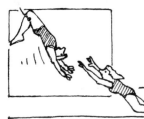

Blindfold Lead.

STAGE 1. In pairs — the seeing partner acts as a guide giving verbal directions on a tour around various indoor/outdoor locations.

STAGE 2. As above but without the securing hand on the shoulder. Also explore tactile experiences —— bark of tree etc.

Circle Up.

Blindfold Walk.

Starting about 15 cms. from the wall, walk 20 paces in a straight line.

Now take 20 paces back to the wall — blindfolded! (The walker will almost certainly stop well short)

Try again. This time the group are there to catch you.

Blindfold Run.

Run full tilt at the group (blindfolded). They will catch you.

If the runner stops short.....

.... start them off closer - walking

.... building up in stages to running again.

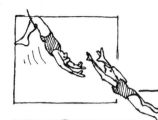

Trust Fall.

In 3s, the middle person stands rigid & is pushed to & fro.

In a circle, taking turns the middle person is rocked around the group.

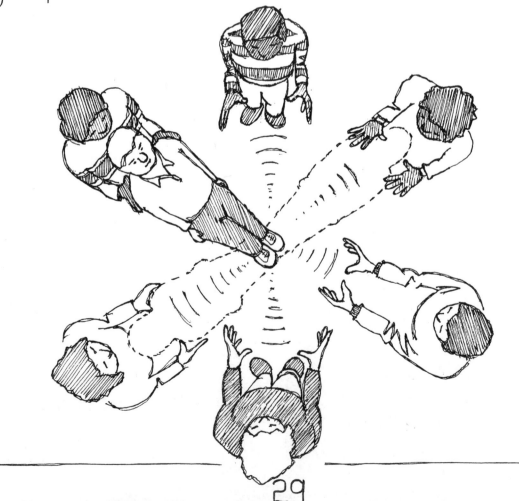

Trust Lift.

1. An exercise for 10 people. The group are going to lift the person lying on the ground above their heads.

One person to support head.

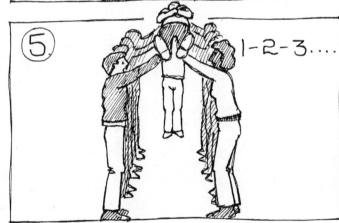

1-2-3....

....Arms drop to this position.

Balancing Act.

A pole or log is suspended from the branch of a tree.

The group must get onto the log....

....& stay on for 1 minute.

Communication.

When things go wrong within organizations, a communication breakdown or an ineffective communication system is very often identified as a major factor.

This section provides a variety of opportunities to explore some of the different methods of communication

Baton Talk.

In turns, the first person, holding a baton, describes a recent event in their lives (e.g. a holiday) for 2 minutes.

The baton is then passed to the next person who must summarize the first account & then tell their own. Check that the summaries include all the main points.

Shields.

Cut out paper shields (one per person). Divide each shield into sections. Title each section with popular topics.

NAME.	FAVOURITE COLOUR.
FAVOURITE SPORT.	PERSON I LIKE BEST.
BEST SONG.	FAVOURITE GROUP.
LIKES.	DISLIKES.

Each person takes a shield & completes the details.

Shields are displayed for general viewing & discussion.

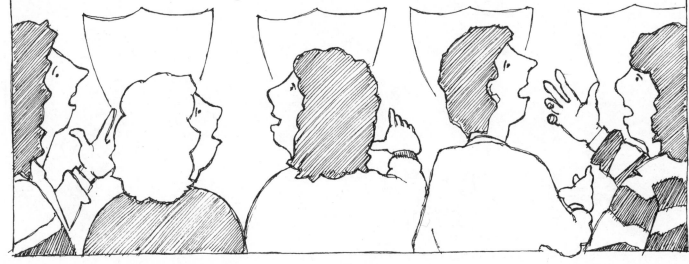

Ball of String Debate.

1. The group are given a subject to debate for 5 minutes.

2. One person holding a ball of string starts.

3. The next person to speak is handed the ball, the first person retains one 'end'.

4. This process is repeated each time someone speaks.

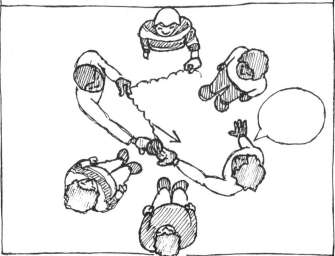

5. Later....

Map of Britain.

This end of the room represents the North coast of Scotland & the far end is the South coast of England. Each person is given the name of a different city. They must arrange themselves geographically on the imaginary map.

Much negotiation & cooperation is required to complete the exercise.

Animal Farm.

Everybody is blindfolded while standing in a line. The name of a different animal is whispered into the ear of each person. (Select ones which make distinctive sounds)

The group now arrange themselves in order of animal size — communication is through the relevant animal sound only.

Now try a similar exercise using numbers instead of animal sounds. When ready blindfolds are removed & animal names & numbers are identified.

Body Language.

1. In turns around the group. One person takes a card & ....

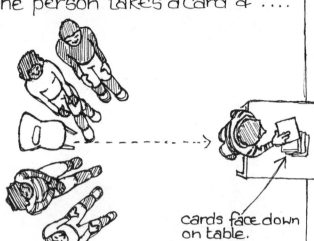

cards face down on table.

2. .... returns it to the bottom of the pile.

ANGER.

3. Only the part of the body indicated may be used to express the emotion to the group —without talking.

hate.?

anger?

4. The next person takes a card & so on.

Sorrow ?

SADNESS.

5.

Friendship ?

Sympathy

SYMPATHY

Use 2 people.

6.

happy?

JOY

The whole body.

38

Blindfold Sheep.

1. All but 1 person is to be blindfolded (the sheep). The sighted person (shepherd) directs the sheep around a course.

2. But first the group are given 5 minutes to devise their own language using sounds. — The shepherd must not use words or numbers as commands.

eg. 1 whistle — start
2 whistles — stop
3 whistles — turn left
4 whistles — turn right.

3. The 'sheep' are now blindfolded & taken into the 'field' areas where they are randomly distributed.

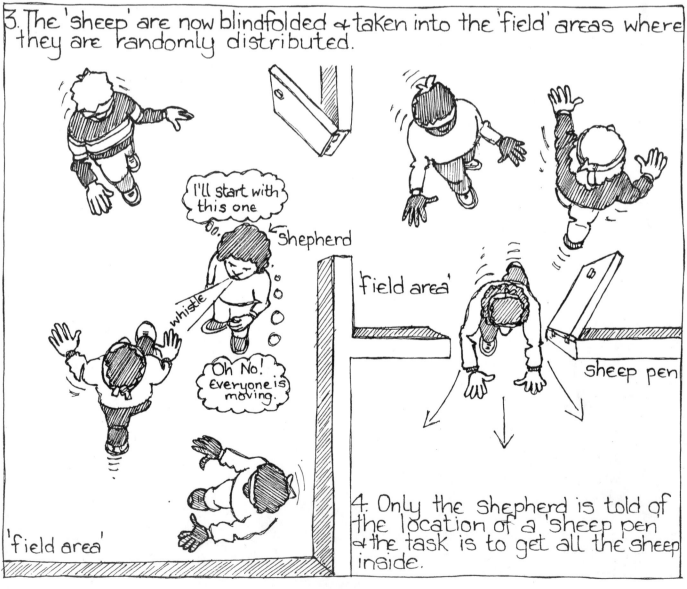

4. Only the shepherd is told of the location of a 'sheep pen' & the task is to get all the sheep inside.

Robot Race.

1. In teams of 3, a blindfolded person from each team — 'the robot' is directed to retrieve a remote box before the robots of the opposing teams.

Each person has a specialised function.

DIRECTOR: — Sees all but cannot speak or move from the spot. Uses hand signals.

CALLER: — Can speak in code but only sees the Director. Cannot move.

ROBOT: — Can hear & is mobile. Cannot see or speak.

Remote Box.

2. Each team has 5 minutes to invent its own coded language of words, sounds & hand signals in order to direct the robot.

GO AHEAD. — WHIPPER

STOP. — POW

RIGHT. — ZING

LEFT. — ZAR.

3. Not allowed: — numbers, or words that have the same first letter as the real word eg: Swish for Stop.

GO AHEAD = WHIPPER = GO AHEAD.

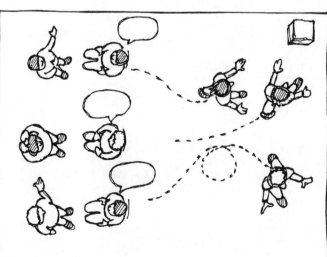

Night Line.

1. The group is blindfolded & tied together in a chain.

2. By touch, they follow a string line around a pre-set course, the leading person giving directions.

3. The line is strung around various points, up & down hills, through undergrowth & so on.

there's a dip ahead.

slow down.

something's caught my foot.

An indoor line with added obstacles.

Night Line Survey.

The group are divided into 'surveyors' & 'mappers'. The surveyors travel the line blindfolded & report information to the mappers who produce a detailed map, in a location out of sight of the line.

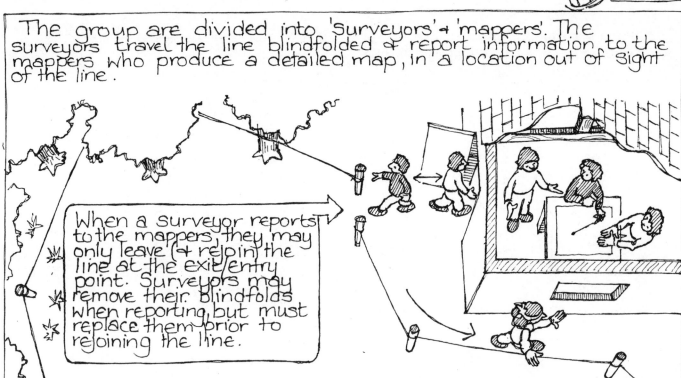

When a surveyor reports to the mappers, they may only leave (& rejoin) the line at the exit/entry point. Surveyors may remove their blindfolds when reporting, but must replace them prior to rejoining the line.

We could have 2 survey teams operating in opposite directions.

Map Room.

Let's try & identify the terrain.

The line travels 6 metres to a post along a gravel path.

Stompers.

Loops of rope, 1 for each person are strung out along 2 planks, alternating from side to side.

Keeping on the planks move 3 metres in a straight line.

Right side, lift together— —2—3—4.

Try a 90° turn.

hang on!

43

Blindfold Tent.

1. Blindfolded participants pitch a tent under the direction of 1 seeing person who is pre-selected from the group.

2. Hand signals are useless....

3. ....so the director must give clear verbal instructions....

STOP!

4. .....& resist the temptation to lend a hand.

5. The blindfolds may only be removed after the tent is pitched.

No Power.

1. Your task is to produce a map of a room including an inventory of all the usable items.

2. Only 10 minutes may be spent in the room to be surveyed & anyone entering must be blindfolded.

3. A discussion ensues involving the different perceptions around the group.

4. This can be checked with a view of the room unblindfolded, once the task is complete.

Blindroom Survey.

The group produce to scale a detailed plan of the contents of a room. Half of the group are blindfolded & remain in the room to be surveyed. The remainder produce the plan in a separate room.

Communication is via the trainer.

This feels like a desk.

There's a desk over here too

Let's get a general list of the contents.

Ask them to pace out the dimensions of the room.

The chair is about 45° to the backwall

Is the chair on the same wall as the desk?

Hierarchy.

1. The group is divided into 3 sub-groups — 'Bosses', 'Workers' & 'Supervisors'. I shall then ask the bosses to erect 4 tents in a set pattern within a time limit of 45 minutes.

BOSSES. —are situated in a remote location & only they receive information about the task.

SUPERVISORS. —pass on verbal directions to the workers & report to the bosses on progress.

WORKERS. —handle equipment.

BOARDROOM · PLAN OF TENTS.

2.

We'll get them to erect one tent first.

SHOP FLOOR

3.

Collect 4 tents & a compass.

4.

There are 3 tent pegs missing.

5. The next tent must point 60°s

Hang on! We haven't got this one up yet.

Street Orienteering.

    This section introduces the concept of maps for younger groups, and provides 6 variations on the theme of street navigation; developing self-reliance, logic and local knowledge.

    ALL that is required is to explore the possibilities in your local area, and to adapt the following exercises accordingly.

Cut Up Map.

1. Preparation: 2 maps are cut into pieces like a jigsaw.

2. 2-3 pieces of each map are placed into envelopes, 1 per person. The pieces in each envelope should belong to the same map.

Each person is handed an envelope.

3. Everybody is instructed to open their envelopes. 2 sub-groups are created as the maps are reformed.

4. Once the maps are reformed, an orienteering exercise may follow.

5. Some method of holding completed maps together e.g. sellotape might be useful.

Local Trail.

This exercise demonstrates how local features can be used as control points in a street orienteering course.

Participants are given a list of instructions to follow & must write down the answers to certain questions as they proceed.

e.g.

START: At the front door ...... turn left onto the nearest road. At the 'T' junction turn right. Take the 2nd road on the right.

① How many lamp posts are there in this road? Turn left at the end of the road & take the first on the right.

② Name the road . . . . Opposite the shops bear left & then 1st right.

⑭ How many drains are on the left side of this road?

From here take the shortest way back to the start.

51

Compass Trail.

In 'Compass Trail' directions are given at road junctions in the form of a compass bearing. Questions about local features are used as control points.

START: At the mainline railway bridge in Albany Road proceed to the crossroads & then follow a bearing of 180°; take the first right.

Q.1. What is the number of the fire hydrant?

Q.2. What is the number of the 2nd house on the right? Proceed to the 'T' junction, then follow a bearing of 0°.

Q.3. What is the number of the post box? At the next junction follow a bearing of 90°.

Q.4. Name the 2nd house on the left. Follow a bearing of 180° at the next junction.

Q.5. What number bus comes along this road?

City Trail.

City Trail provides a list of questions relating to various landmarks & features. This exercise does not provide directions or a map so some familiarity with the City Centre is useful.

START: At the Juvenile Court.

1. When was the Church of the Greyfriars built?

2. Between the Bullyard & Shelton Square, look up. Who killed the Duncow?

3. Go to the Birdcage Arcade — What 3 animals can you see?

4. Towards the train station is a statue of James Starley — When did he invent the bicycle?

5. Go to Ford's Hospital — When was it founded?

Photo Trail I.

Participants are given a map & a list of various features & landmarks to locate & photograph. The map is marked with dots to indicate the general location but not the identity of the feature.

Make the task more difficult by blanking out all the road names on the map.

The developed photographs can be matched against a set showing the correct features

LOCATE & PHOTOGRAPH THE FOLLOWING
Factory chimney, Norman Tower, Statue, M 6 , Birds on lake, Stile, etc., ...

M.6

PhotoTrail II.

A trail, which is navigated by following a set of photographs, is set around unfamiliar streets. Each photograph identifies a different feature along the route & all must be located in order to reach the finishing point. The photographs are not presented in order & only half of them are numbered. The photograph marking the finish should not be numbered.

Start off the participants within sight of the location shown in the first picture.

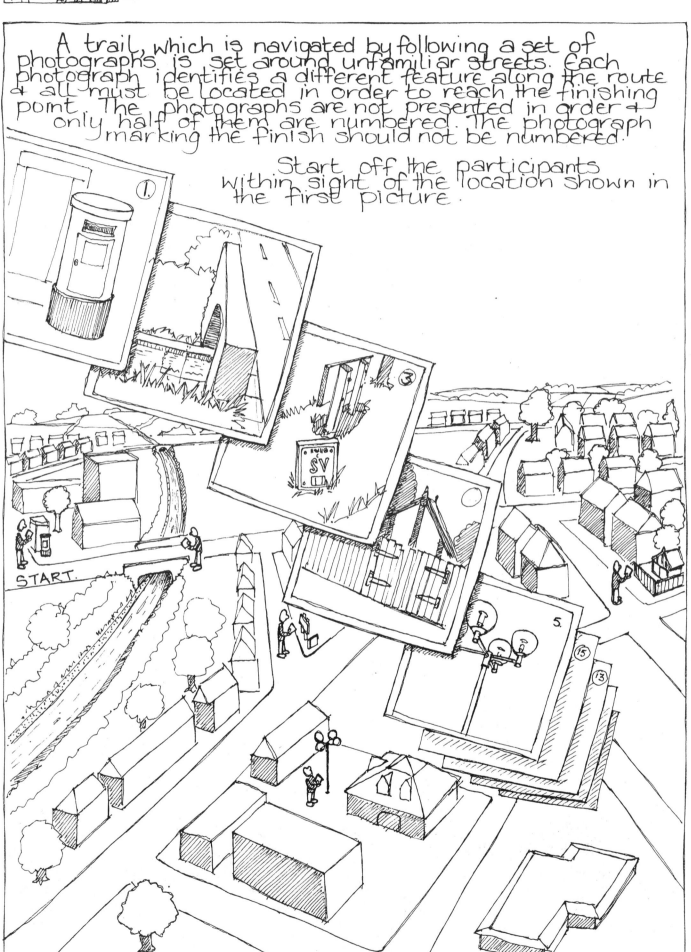

Blank Map.

The group are taken to an unfamiliar town & dropped off individually at separate locations. Each person receives a street map with all the road names blanked out.

A 'YOU ARE HERE' sign marks the appropriate drop off point. The only other position indicated is the finish, where transport home is waiting.

Include a 'fail safe' landmark which is easily located for use in the event of someone getting lost.

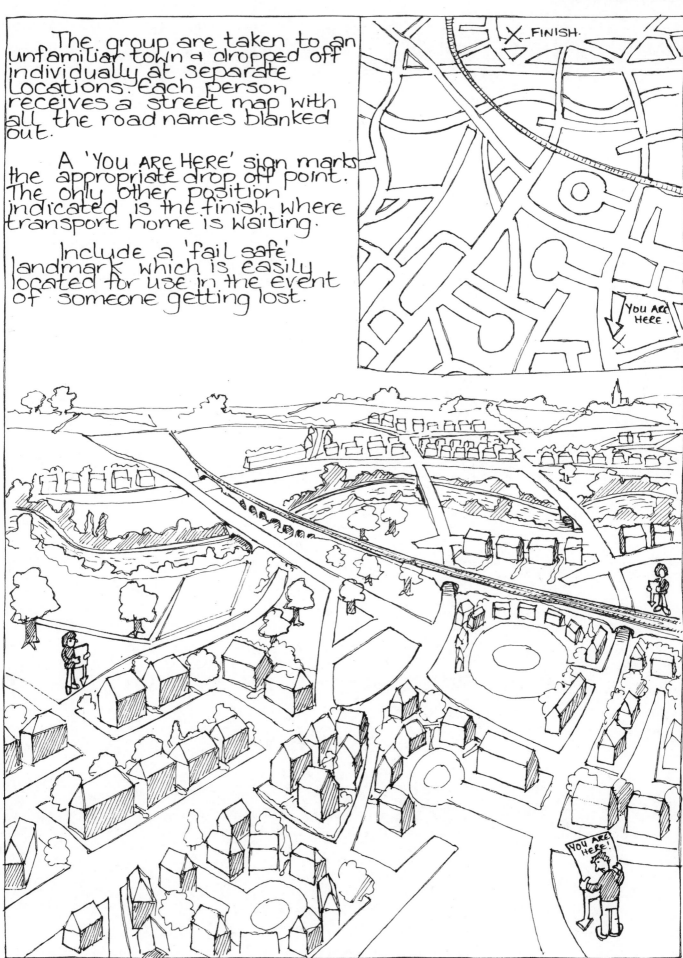

Problem Solving.

Here is a range of activities that test ingenuity, logic, imagination, cooperation and organization. The problems take the form of either crossing an obstacle, retrieving an inaccessible object or a construction exercise.

Some of the problems have a specific answer, rather like a puzzle with success or failure being relatively clear, whilst others have any number of possible solutions.

These exercises can be linked together to form a series of problems.

The equipment that is shown for each activity is the minimum required to solve the problem. The addition of extra bits and pieces of irrelevant equipment can be used to further complicate the exercise with advanced groups— see Labrynth on page 68

Acid River

1. A competitive exercise for 2 teams of equal numbers. Both teams must cross from A to B without touching the ground. The first team across wins. Each team is given 2 blocks of wood.

If any person touches the acid river they must return to the start.

4. let's borrow your shoe laces.

8. In the non-competitive version the whole group must cross in a time limit.

Minefield.

① 2 tyres are suspended about 50 cms. above the ground from the branch of a tree, in the middle of the 'minefield'. 2 planks are supplied to the group.

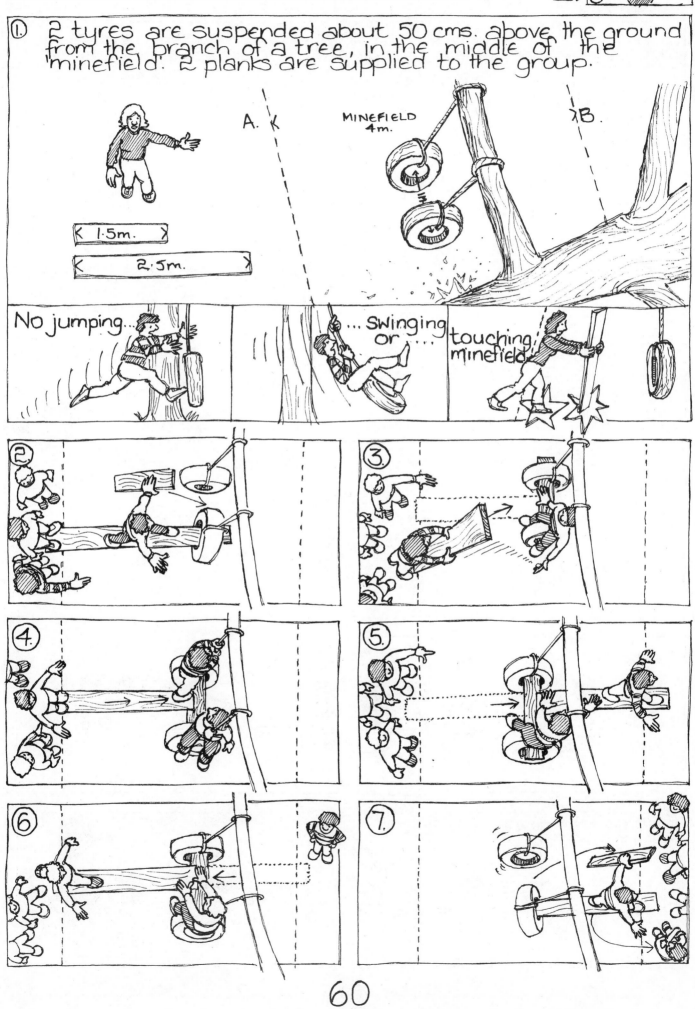

A.

MINEFIELD
4m.

B.

1.5m.

2.5m.

No jumping... ...Swinging or ... touching minefield.

②

③

④

⑤

⑥

⑦

Shark Island.

Cross from Island A to Island C. A plank is provided but is too short to bridge the gaps between islands.

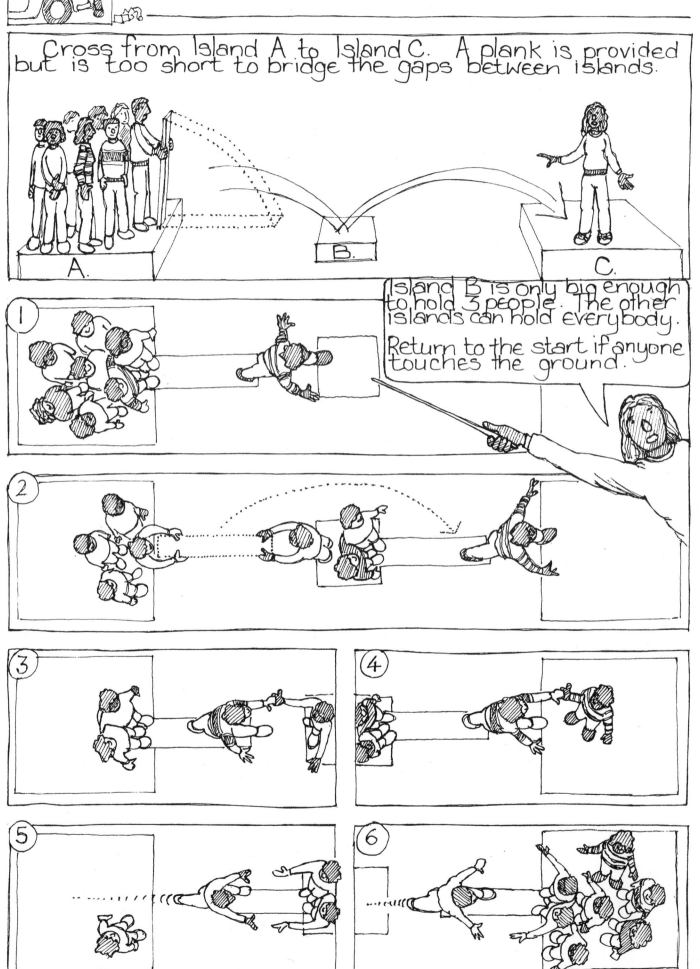

Crocodile River.

3 oil drums & 2 wooden planks are used in this crossing. The oil drums & planks must reach this side with the group. (Milk crates may be substituted for oil drums.)

If any person or plank touches the river the whole team must return to the start.

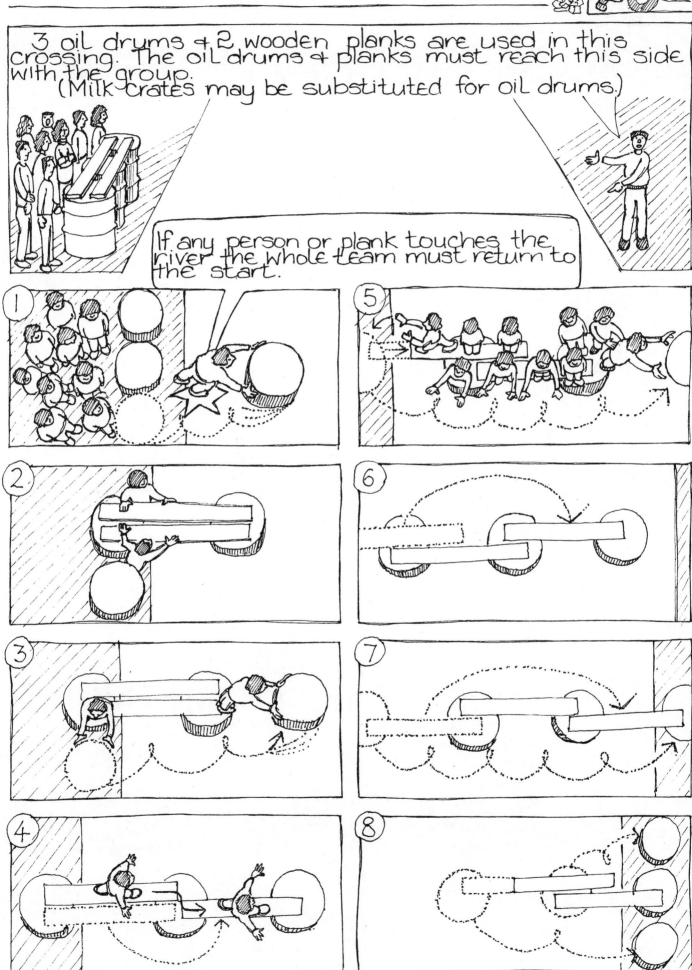

Stepping Stones.

1. 8 upturned waste paper bins act as stepping stones. 4 planks of 2 different lengths are provided; A. & B. are 2 metres & C & D are 1.5 metres. All the planks must reach the opposite side with the team!

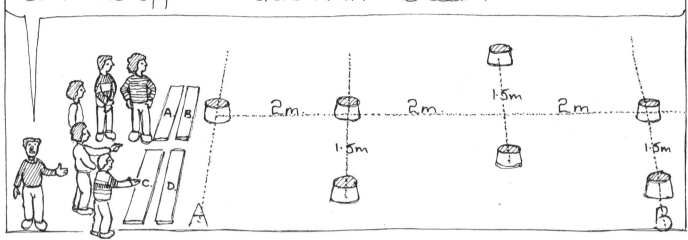

2m   2m   1.5m   2m

1.5m   1.5m   1.5m

2. 2 & 1.5 metre planks are always laid at 90° to each other – like so.

3. Planks are picked up & then re-laid.

4.

5. It is possible to retrieve all the planks from this position.

Ravine.

2 poles have been laid across a ditch & are fixed into position; being wider apart on the far bank. 8 equal length planks of wood are used to build a bridge.

All the planks must end up on the far bank with the group.

1.

2. It is possible to lay the first plank across the poles. The gap then becomes too wide.

3. The planks are laid out in a herringbone pattern.

4. Before we can retrieve the planks, the pattern must be re-laid from this side.

5. From this position all the planks can be picked up & taken across.

Matrix.

The matrix is an 8x8 square grid. 1 square is marked as the entry & another is marked as the exit. The matrix can be drawn in chalk or made out of string & pegged out on grass. The group must work out the route across, within a time limit.

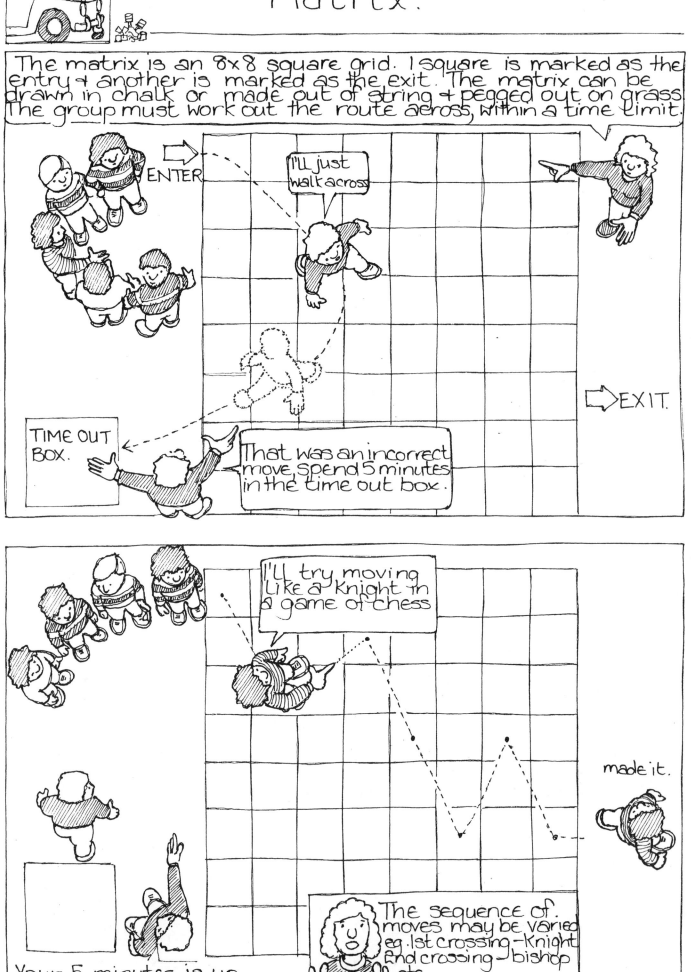

ENTER

I'll just walk across

EXIT.

TIME OUT BOX.

That was an incorrect move, spend 5 minutes in the time out box.

I'll try moving like a Knight in a game of chess

made it.

Your 5 minutes is up, rejoin the group.

The sequence of moves may be varied eg. 1st crossing - Knight 2nd crossing - bishop etc..

Laser.

Retrieve the box in the centre of the 2 squares. Both squares are protected by lasers which can be deactivated by removing the 2 fuses located on the top of the box & bringing them outside the squares.

OUTER SQUARE

INNER SQUARE

Broom pole.

2 plastic collars made from a washing up liquid bottle.

Remove fuse 1 to de-activate the inner square, & fuse 2 to de-activate the outer.

Your equipment is a ball of string.

Cardboard box.

FUSE 1.

FUSE 2

CONTINUED.....

Laser.

1

2

3

...tie a
slip knot.

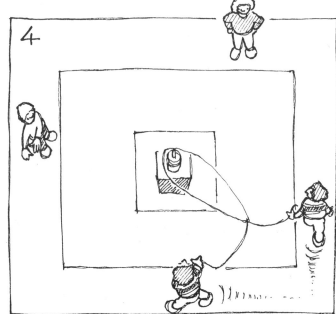

4

5

6

67

Labyrinth.

Labyrinth, combines the Matrix & Laser exercises. The group are locked into a perimeter path surrounding the laser field. The only way out is through a matrix. The group is divided into 2 units each restricted to opposite sides of the path. Consequently, once the box has been retrieved, each unit must exit through a separate matrix.

I've added a coat hanger, milk crate & a plank to the equipment.

The group have ½ hour to complete the exercise.

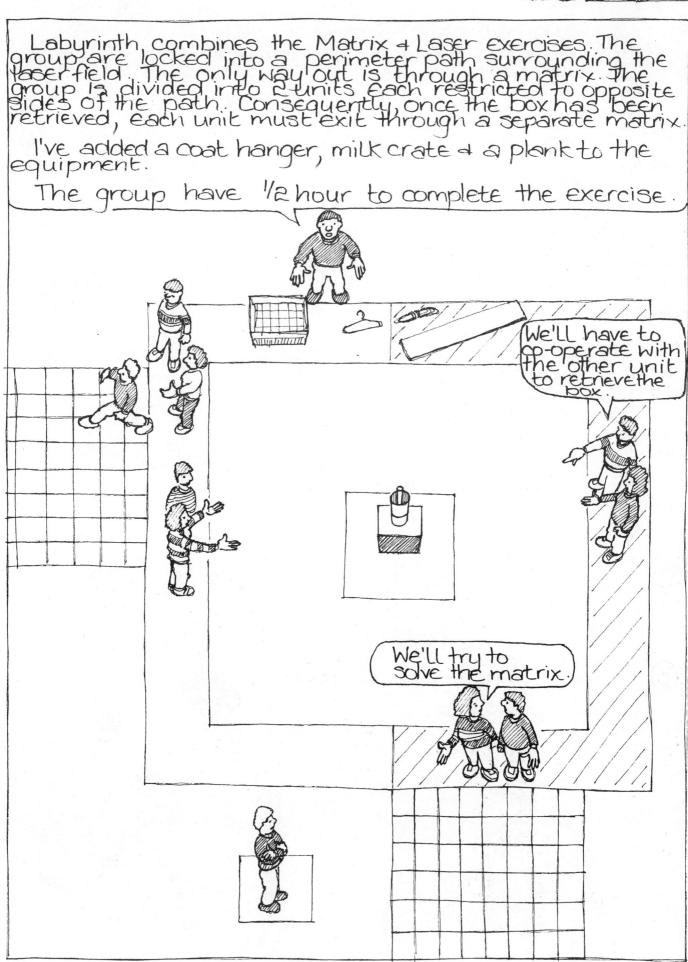

Minefield II

Tyre Change.

Retrieve the tyre.

Select the size of tyre (car/lorry) + height of pole according to the ability of the group.

Note how the uninvolved in this exercise move to the edge of the group.

Electric Fence.

① You have 20 minutes to retrieve the box. All must stay this side of the fence. You will incur a 5 minute penalty if any person or item of equipment comes into contact with the fence.

Heavy box with handle e.g 'ammo box'.

string

Plastic tube - 2 metres.

Pen knife

71

Stoves.

The separated parts of 2 multi-element camping stoves are placed in a box, together with the ingredients for making a drink (tea/coffee) or a simple meal.

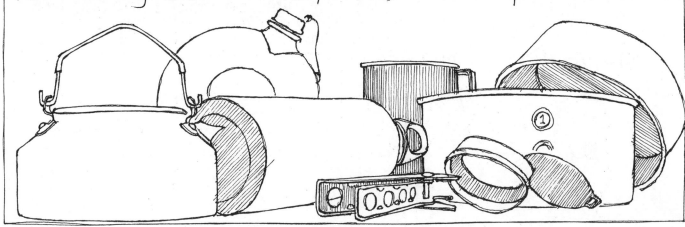

A stove must be assembled to the cooking position & the drink prepared. Finally the stoves must be reassembled in the packed position.

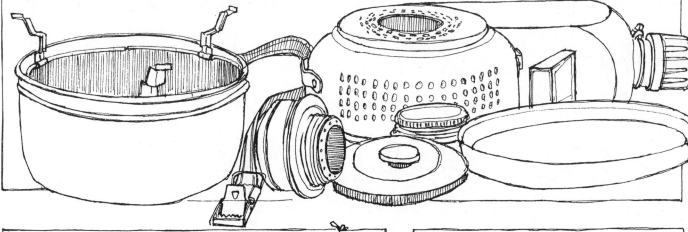

Don't!

An instructor should advise on safety.

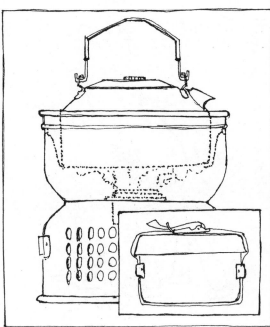

Whizz Planes Ltd.

73

Under the Bridge.

① Pass a bucket of water under the bridge without spilling any. Stay in the middle of the bridge & do not come into direct contact with the water during the exercise.

Bottle

Bucket

2 ropes.

Karabiner or weight

string

②

string

③

④

⑤

⑥

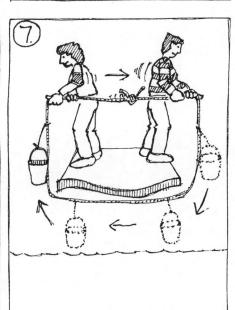

⑦

Propel an Egg.

1. Your task is to propel this egg a distance of 8 metres through the air in one movement, & without breaking it. You may only use the items on the table to assist you. Plan what you do & be imaginative.

Chariots Of Fire.

Using only the equipment on the table, propel a lit candle as far as possible. Time & distance trials will begin when you have devised your propulsion method.

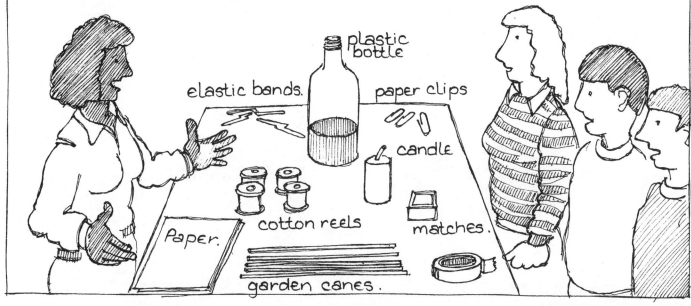

Organization.

These activities are constructed in such a way that the best results are only achieved if the participants are well organized and work together.

They range from a simple survey which can be carried out indoors, e.g. 'shoe-lace survey' on page 79, to a more difficult obstacle course that demands a high level of co-operation, without which the exercise cannot be completed, — see 'Obstacle Course 3' on page 89

Some preparation is required for the more complex games together with a few simple items of equipment such as old car tyres and ropes.

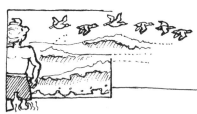

Shoe Lace Survey.

A simple introduction to Organizational Games ; all that is required is a pencil & paper & that someone should be wearing lace-up shoes. Irregular shaped rooms with high ceilings make the task more difficult.

The group is given 10 minutes to work out the volume of the room in cubic shoe laces. Afterwards, discuss who did what?, what degree of accuracy did they adopt?, & was everybody involved?

Squares.

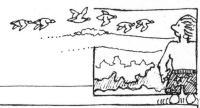

1. The whole team must get inside the square & hold their position for 30 seconds.

chalk square

Draw the square so that it is too small for the whole group to stand in it.

2. Only 1 person is allowed to survey the square.

I'll pace it out.....

3. It's about this big...

4. The group have 5 minutes to practise away from the square.

5. LATER...

We're ready

6. They only get 1 attempt.

Blindfold Square.

1. A loop of rope is placed on the ground & the group is blindfolded.

2. Everybody take hold of the rope & try to form a square.

Let's start with 4 people to act as the corners.

3. If the corners take the rope around their backs it is easier to make a right angle.

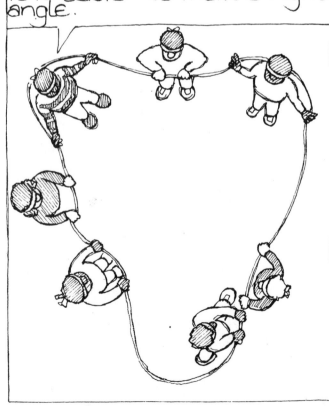

4. When you think you're ready shout out but hold your position.

81

Reef Knot.

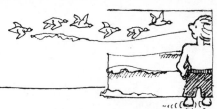

① Everybody take hold of the rope, now tie a knot around the pole without letting go.

② We'll need to plan this first.

③ left over right & under.

④

The knot should be tied as tight as possible.

The Spider's Web.

A network of string is suspended from the branch of a tree (or ceiling). Everyone must get through the web without touching it.

Any hole in the web may only be used once, i.e one person only through each hole — so the task gets progressively more difficult.

The Spider's Web.

The design of each web can be varied according to the size & ability of the group.

If any person touches the web either they or the whole team must return to the start. Alternatively apply point or time penalties.

① The group is divided into 3 'High Tech' & 2 'Low Tech' units. The units aim to earn as many tokens as possible by producing & selling geometric shapes out of paper to the instructor.

② 'High Tech' units have 'Technology' (as illustrated) & 20 tokens each to start with...

③ ...& 'Low Tech' units only have raw materials (lots of newspapers etc) & 5 tokens each.

④ The instructor sets the shape to be produced by all units in each production phase which lasts for 5 minutes.

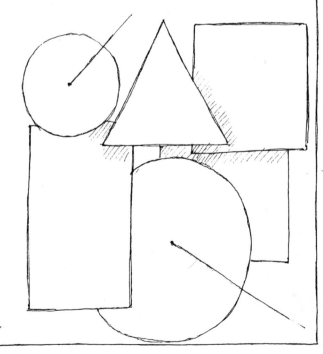

⑤ Extra equipment can be purchased at any stage – eg. ruler, compass, scissors, at a cost of 20 tokens each. Paper costs 1 token for 2 sheets

I'll pay 5 tokens for each good 3" circle.

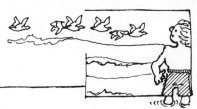

Obstacle Course II.

A 'string line' is taken around various obstacles to create a circuit.

The team earn a point for each circuit that is completed by 'any' person. A time limit is set depending on the size & difficulty of the course

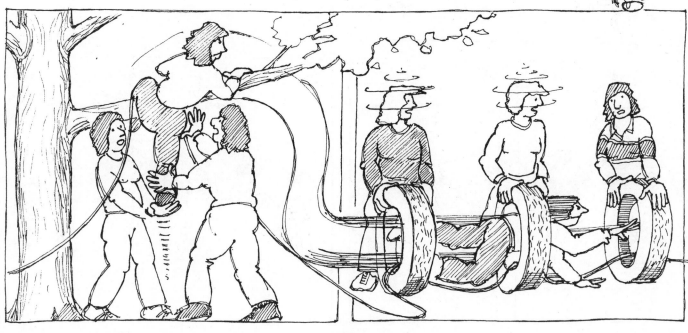

Complex Games.

Each 'complex game' is comprised of different problem elements which must be resolved before the final objective can be achieved. They build on many of the themes from the previous sections and provide several hours of activity.

All require some preparation and a certain amount of adaptation according to local conditions.

The wooden puzzle box in 'Danger UX2' is the only sophisticated item of equipment required throughout this book. Construction details are supplied on page 98-99. The initial effort in building will be rewarded by the interest generated as groups try to open it.

Urban Journey

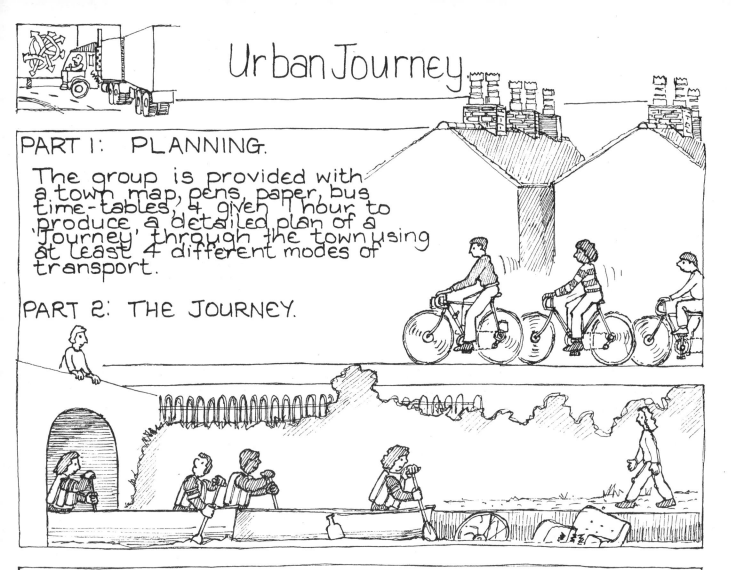

PART 1: PLANNING.

The group is provided with a town map, pens, paper, bus time-tables, & given 1 hour to produce a detailed plan of a 'Journey' through the town using at least 4 different modes of transport.

PART 2: THE JOURNEY.

RULES:

1) The journey must begin & end at a predetermined point.

2) Cars, motorbikes or minibus are excluded.

3) The route must cover 4 miles within a set time.

4) No place to be visited more than once.

5) Climbing or canoeing equipment may only be used under the supervision of an instructor who will transport the equipment as directed.

6) A small cash float is available.

EXAMPLE OF ROUTE PLAN:

5:00 – 5:10 p.m. Walk to Highway.

5:10 – 5:20. Catch № 27 bus to Canal Bridge.

5:20 – 5:45. Abseil off bridge.

5:45 – 6:20. Canoe 2 miles of canal etc.......

Chemical Busters.

A navigation exercise around 9 control points on an orienteering course; the task being to collect a number of sealed boxes containing food & drink, and pieces of written information, that are distributed around the course.

The group is first given the instructions as set out below together with an orienteering map.

A mad scientist has placed a number of dangerous chemicals, contained in cardboard boxes labelled A to E, around the park.

The task is to find them & remove them to a mixing site where they must be safely disposed of.

A map of the area indicates the location of the hidden chemicals.

Proceed to Point 30 on the map where further instructions are given.

Continued....

Chemical Busters.

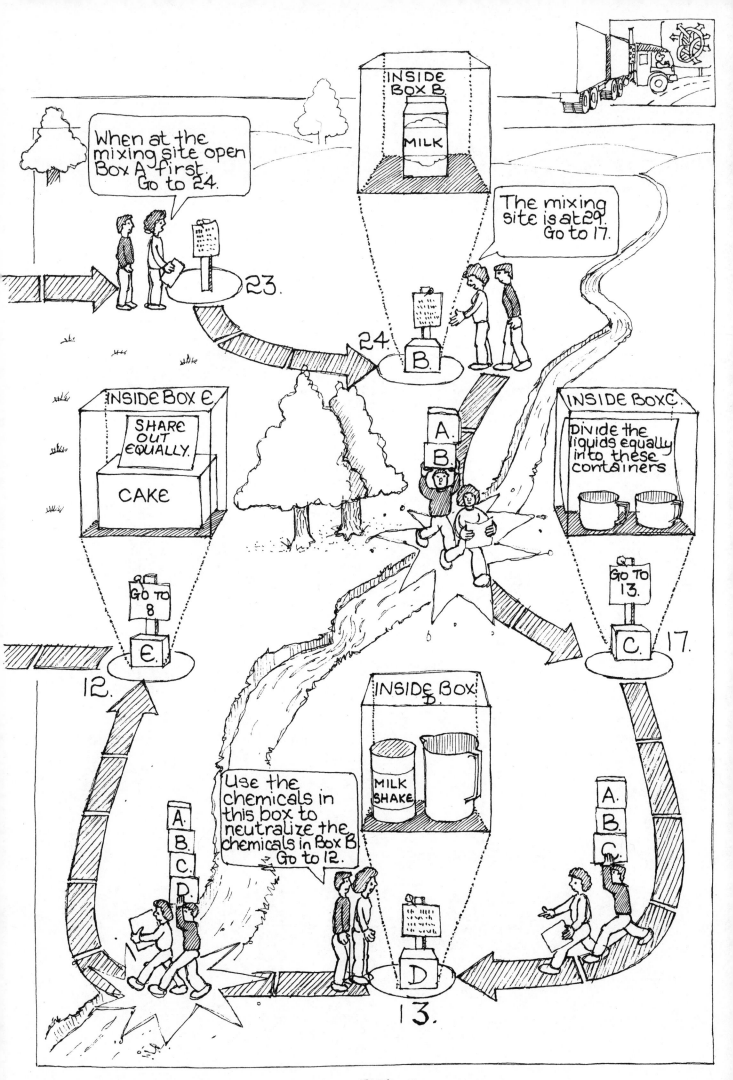

Make 'Chemical Busters' more challenging by adding various problem solving exercises which must be resolved in order to retrieve the boxes.

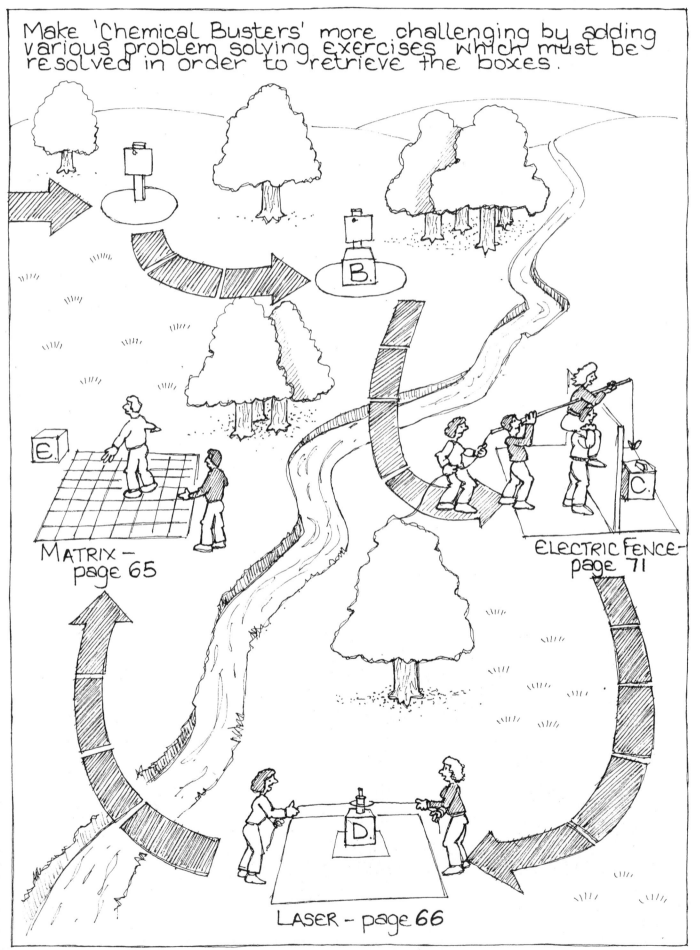

MATRIX — page 65

ELECTRIC FENCE — page 71

LASER — page 66

95

Danger U.X.2.

1. UXP is a wooden box containing a reward, e.g. a cake, which can only be retrieved by following a 6 stage unlocking sequence.

If it is not followed exactly a destruct mechanism is activated.

The box can be constructed from basic materials - see following pages.

DO NOT MOVE THIS BOX IS SET TO DESTROY ITS CONTENTS IF OPENED INCORRECTLY.

SOAPY WATER.

CAKE.

2. Step by step instructions for opening the box are concealed within an information gathering/problem solving exercise.

STEP 3.

STEP 4.

STEP 5.

STEP 1.

STEP 6 Remove pin from.....

STEP 2.

LOCKED POSITION.

A system of removable 6" nails, holes & slots form a locking mechanism. It supports 2 hinged flaps & a loop of string which holds a container of soapy water.

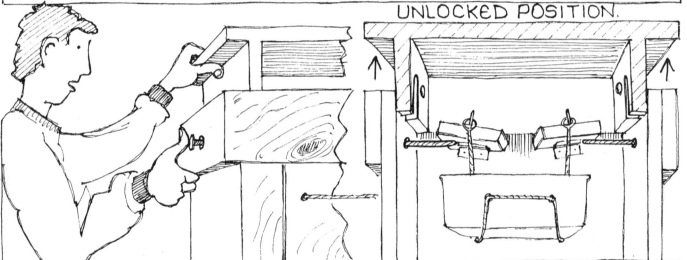

UNLOCKED POSITION.

If the nails are swopped around in the correct sequence they will continue to support the flaps while releasing the lid which can then be removed & the box 'disarmed'.

Whoops!

Splash!

If a nail is incorrectly removed, a flap will be released & the reward ruined.

U.X.2.

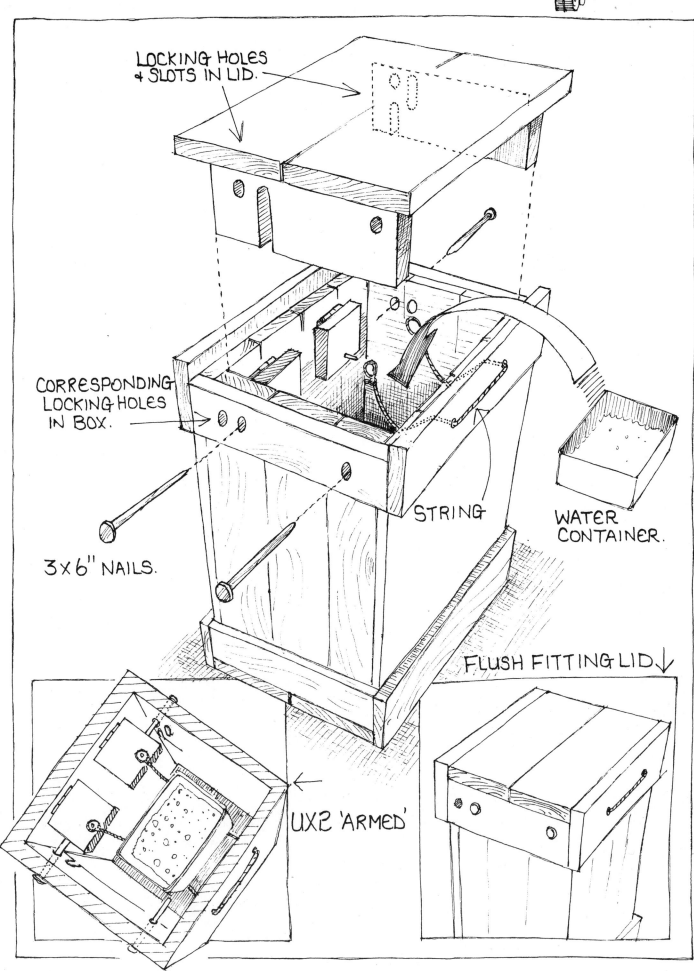

LOCKING HOLES & SLOTS IN LID.

CORRESPONDING LOCKING HOLES IN BOX.

3 x 6" NAILS.

STRING

WATER CONTAINER.

FLUSH FITTING LID ↓

UX2 'ARMED'

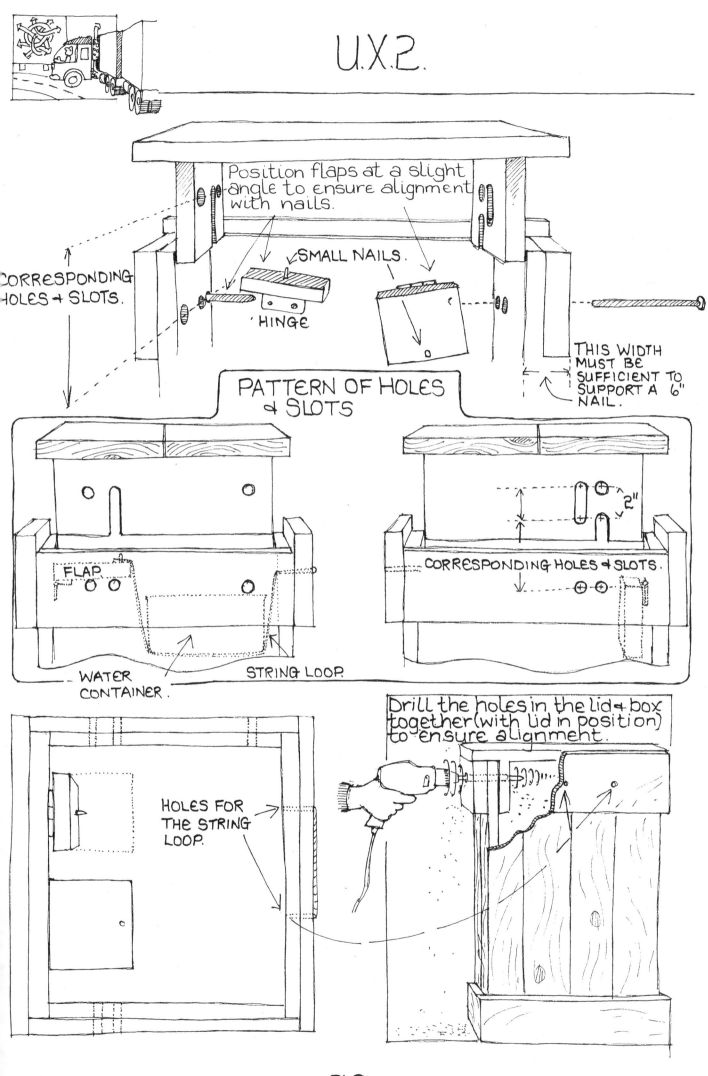

Position flaps at a slight angle to ensure alignment with nails.

SMALL NAILS.

CORRESPONDING HOLES & SLOTS.

HINGE

THIS WIDTH MUST BE SUFFICIENT TO SUPPORT A 6" NAIL.

PATTERN OF HOLES & SLOTS

2"

CORRESPONDING HOLES & SLOTS.

FLAP

WATER CONTAINER.

STRING LOOP.

HOLES FOR THE STRING LOOP.

Drill the holes in the lid & box together (with lid in position) to ensure alignment.

U.X.2.

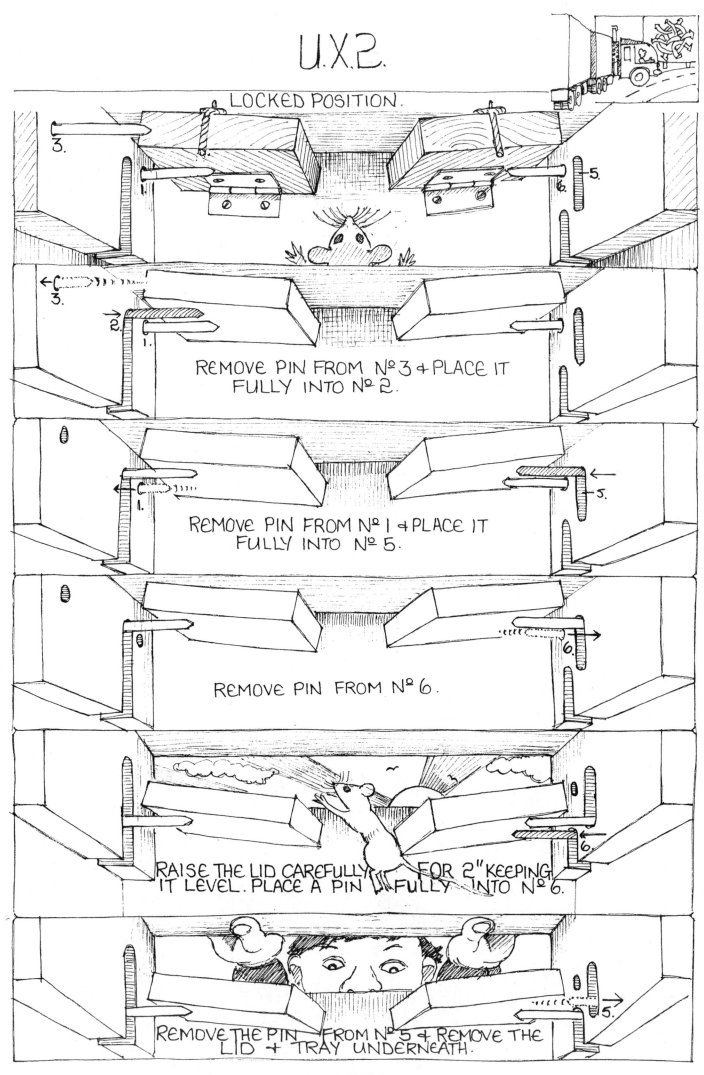

LOCKED POSITION.

REMOVE PIN FROM Nº 3 & PLACE IT
FULLY INTO Nº 2.

REMOVE PIN FROM Nº 1 & PLACE IT
FULLY INTO Nº 5.

REMOVE PIN FROM Nº 6.

RAISE THE LID CAREFULLY FOR 2" KEEPING
IT LEVEL. PLACE A PIN FULLY INTO Nº 6.

REMOVE THE PIN FROM Nº 5 & REMOVE THE
LID & TRAY UNDERNEATH.

Challenge.

READ THE INSTRUCTIONS.

Juggle 3 balls in the air for 30 seconds. ⭐ 5.

Keep a football in the air by 'heading it'. ALL members of the group must head the ball twice ⭐ 10.

Stay under water for 30 seconds. ⭐ 5.

INSTRUCTIONS.

The objective is to score 100 points by completing any of the tasks illustrated. Each task has a certain points value eg. ⭐5 which is awarded after it has been successfully completed.

Points have to be used to hire the transport necessary to complete certain tasks.

You may practice a task as often as you like but you are only allowed 1 official attempt.

All of the necessary equipment is contained in the box.

You have 10 points to start with.

⭐ 20. Get the whole group up to 200m. above sea level.

⭐ 20. Collect the letters from 3 control posts of an orienteering course. 5

⭐ 20. Cross a stream at 2 different points at least 200m. apart. TIME LIMIT 4½ MINS.

NOTE: SET THE TRANSPORT TO COST ABOUT 30 POINTS OVERALL.

THE FOLLOWING TASKS REQUIRE TRANSPORT

Challenge.

At precisely 6:15pm gather the group together & all shout.....

.... a topical phrase....

★ 5.

What is the Welsh word for Wales? ★ 5.

Produce a completed crossword from today's newspaper. ★ 5.

Propel a raw egg 14 metres through the air & return it undamaged. ★ 10.

1 extra egg is available at a cost of 5 points.

EQUIPMENT BOX — containing playing cards, 2 raw eggs, 3 empty bottles, 3 dinner knives, cup, today's newspaper, bucket, football, 3 tennis balls, pen & paper, orienteering map, local O.S. map & ruler.

Write down the name of each group member before attempting any of the other tasks or lose 10 points. ★ 5.

Build a playing card tower at least 15" high. ★ 10.

What is the name of the nearest campsite? ★ 5.

What is the number of the nearest public telephone box? ★ 5.

Place 3 bottles more than a knife's distance apart. Balance a structure of 3 knives on the bottles to support a cupful of water. ★ 10.

103

Review.

PLAN.   DO.   REVIEW.

Blindfold Review.

1. Some people may be too afraid to speak their mind during the review.

2. This exercise ensures that everyone says what they think. Everybody stands in a line & puts on blindfolds.

3. Individuals are now instructed either to take paces forwards or backwards depending on how they feel about the performance of the group without talking i.e.

1 pace forward — fair

2 paces forward — good

etc. . . . .

1 pace backwards — poor

2 paces backward — Very poor

etc. . . . .

4. Each person explains the reasons for their chosen position while staying in place.

Auto-Review.

The group are asked to imagine they collectively form a car with each person representing a different part. This is followed by a discussion of each person's role in the group.

Pete — the engine — he has lots of energy.

Phil — the tyres — everybody seems to tread on him (scapegoat)

Marcia — the steering wheel — she's a good leader.

Bill — the bumpers — he is very argumentative.

① Try & get everyone inside the circle that I've drawn in chalk, & stay there for 15 seconds....

②

③ ....try a smaller circle....

....now it's up to you to set your own limits for the smallest possible circle.

④ Use this exercise to examine with the group how they set their objectives — Are they too ambitious or too easy?

Shuffle.

① If a group has become too competitive try this . . . .

Divide them into 3 sub-groups + randomly share out 4 packs of cards between them.

② Tell them, as a group to arrange the cards into suits — by exchanging cards between sub-groups.

Communication is via an instructor.

③ Ask Group B for Clubs.

④ I've just collected clubs. Tell them we haven't got any.

⑤ The sub-groups should not be able to hear each others conversations.

⑥ If they fail to achieve the objective, the reasons can be identified during the review e.g. too selfish.

Epilogue.